袁府驴肉

正宗 特产 袁府™

余水县佳康食品有限公司
话: 0312-8663092 0312-8663095 072

鱷魚肉
CROCODILE MEAT

補虛極品 食中之最
喘咳痛風 消渴糖尿
體弱多病 最宜食用

IT IS GOOD TO EAT
AND BENEFICIAL
TO YOUR HEALTH

泰國是拉差美達有限公司
SRIRACHA MODA CO., LTD.
TEL : 0-3893-8104
FAX : 0-3893-8105

Mfg. Date

Product of Australia

SEAMASTERS
EMU
SOFT JERKY
30g NET

PORK SPLEEN/PACK
ม้าม,ตับเหล็ก/แพ็ค

20405600170002007
ปริมาณสุทธิ   0.200 กก.   หน่วย
วันที่ผลิต   04.12.09
วันที่หมดอายุ   07.12.09 $17.00
บาท/กก.   85.00   (338)   4054

บริษัท ฟู้ดแลนด์ซุปเปอร์มาร์เก็ต จำกัด

YUCK!

Mayu –
some travel and culinary
inspiration for you and
Leo! Wonder how many
of these goodies you've
already tried...
Love,
Meera

YUCK!
the things people eat

NEIL SETCHFIELD

MERRELL
LONDON · NEW YORK

Contents

Introduction

There is but one truth about food: we have to eat it to survive. Whoever we are, wherever we are, our bodies need nutrition of some kind if they are to function properly. In contemporary Western society, it's not particularly difficult to meet that need; indeed, when it comes to satisfying our nutritional requirements we're spoilt for choice. Furthermore, it's generally accepted that what is proffered for sale in restaurants, supermarkets and other food outlets is the norm. In other parts of the world, however, although the need for food is exactly the same, what determines normality is undoubtedly quite different.

In the course of my travels around the world, I have come to realize something that perhaps, subconsciously, I've always known: that, although we in the West act with indignant superiority regarding our food choices, essentially we all eat the same thing. Human beings have eaten and still eat almost every part of every animal, fish and plant they can lay their hands on — provided it's not going to kill them. Whether it be goat's testicles in Indonesia, ox tongue in the United Kingdom or sheep's penis in China, it all boils (or grills or roasts or fries) down to the same thing: flesh. What varies, of course — and what interests me — is the way in which different cultures perceive the same foodstuff.

This book is a light-hearted exploration — in glorious photographic detail — of the idea that the same dish can be seen as perfectly acceptable by some, yet as completely revolting by others; that what one person or nationality might consider distasteful ('Yuck!'), another will regard as delicious ('Yum!'). It also aims to show some 'normal' foodstuffs in a new and unexpected light.

SPIDERS – IT ALL STARTED WITH SPIDERS

Tarantulas, to be exact, stir-fried with garlic and ginger – crispy-legged little beauties with a gooey, black, viscous middle tasting vaguely of … well, goo, to be honest, although some (they're wrong) say crab. At that point, however, I had no idea of what I was getting myself into.

I was travelling in Cambodia, and one night in Phnom Penh, on a whim, I bought a couple of stir-fried tarantulas from a street stall, to photograph rather than to eat. On the way back to my hotel I stopped in a local bar for a drink. The waitresses laughed when they saw what I'd bought and immediately christened me 'Spiderman' – although that didn't stop them from trying to eat my little bag of goodies. From then on they would shout 'Here comes Spiderman!' whenever I passed by.

It was only when I saw the spiders close up, however, through the lens of my camera, that I knew I was on to something. There they were in all their gory detail: heads crushed and oozing; spiky hairs on each of their broken, twisted legs; flakes of garlic speckling their bodies – a sticky, funky, glutinous mess. And I thought: people eat these things? Each night thereafter I'd buy a bag of whatever exotic street snack I could find, and every night in the bar I became the 'Frogman' or 'Snakeman', depending on what I'd purchased. The waitresses thought I was nuts – hell, I thought I was nuts – but I also knew that the images would make a fantastic photo story.

What really appealed to me wasn't so much what these unusual foodstuffs were – although that helped, obviously – as what they looked like through my camera. I was used to shooting the food of Michelin-starred chefs, but nothing could compare to the excitement of capturing the simple, uncomplicated way in which these dishes were presented. It was a world away from so-called fine dining: no foam,

espuma or jus here. It was 'snake on a stick' or 'cow-toenail soup'. Little was left to the imagination — which is as it should be with food. The names of the dishes said simply, 'It's this, cooked this way. Just eat it, or don't.'

Back in London, the general response to my photos was, literally, 'Yuck!' — the complete opposite to that of the Cambodians, who had mostly said 'Yum!' Although I was encouraged by these initial reactions to my culinary discoveries, I quickly realized that I would need more examples and much greater coverage to make the project work: I suspected that 'strange' foods could be found in every corner of the globe, not just on the streets of Cambodia. At a meeting for a completely different book, I mentioned the photos to my publisher, and soon a journey from one surreal culinary landscape to another had really begun.

THERE'S A DOG'S HEAD IN THE MINIBAR

During my travels, photographing the foodstuffs in which I was interested wasn't always straightforward. Some locals — for example, at the dog-meat restaurants in Hanoi, Vietnam — were a little sensitive, a consequence, perhaps, of the Western media's tendency to point accusatory fingers at certain culinary practices. This meant that I had to buy the items in question and take them back to my hotel to photograph. I spent many hours wandering the streets looking like a typical tourist but with shopping bags full of dogs, rats and snakes. Quite what the hotel maid thought of the contents of my minibar I'll never know.

Finding the various foods was also a challenge. Although I researched hard and wide before travelling to each of my destinations, sometimes I just got lucky. Walking through Vientiane in Laos one afternoon, I came across a little old lady selling fresh herbs and fruit. On closer inspection, I noticed that she was also in possession of a pile of smoked rats. I bought a couple, naturally, and she didn't bat an eyelid. Sometimes there was no other way of finding these things.

And then there were the sea monsters. At both Tsukiji Market in Tokyo and Jagalchi Fish Market in Busan, South Korea, I discovered creatures that even now I'm not sure really exist; every bug-eyed, slimy, wriggling scaly beast you could possibly imagine. I happily ate sea squirt and sea cucumber (quite nasty), but turned down dolphin, whale and, in particular, hagfish. Not one of nature's beauties, to say the least, this eel-shaped fish is really, really unpleasant. It lives encased in what can be described only as gloop, a thick, mucous-like slime that acts as a deterrent to predators and photographers alike.

ONE MAN'S 'YUCK!' IS ANOTHER MAN'S 'YUM!'

One of the aims of this book is to demonstrate that, when it comes to food, palatability is highly subjective. I grew up eating what some might consider unpleasant. As a child, my favourite meal was tripe (cow's stomach) and onions, cooked in milk and served with mashed potatoes. For me it was the delicious norm, along with black pudding (blood sausage) and, as an occasional treat, laverbread (puréed seaweed) on toast. (I should, I suppose, mention that I'm Welsh.) Some people, however, turn their noses up at such delightful fare.

Ultimately, how and where a person was brought up will determine their reaction to these pictures: some will start to think about lunch, while others will begin to feel a little queasy. Personally, I hold no

opinions on whether it's right or wrong to consume the foods featured in this book; neither do I wish to put forward a particular political agenda. My hope, rather, is that anyone who looks at these photographs will come away with a more enlightened idea of what constitutes food, and will think twice before getting on their high horse (still eaten in France, by the way) about what others see as a tasty snack, a nutritious meal or merely a means of survival. After all, this isn't a cookery book or an encyclopedia: it's just another way of looking at the things we sometimes take for granted.

A NOTE ON THE TEXT

Each of the following entries comprises the location at which the food was obtained; its name; and a brief description of what it is, where it's eaten — and, in some cases, how to enjoy it at home.

UGLY BUG BALL

Cicadas on a stick

The Dong Hua Men Night Market is something of a Mecca for lovers of unusual foods, attracting tourists and locals alike. Cicadas, whether skewered on a stick or not, are regarded as a delicacy in many parts of China and South-East Asia, including Vietnam and Malaysia.

Beetles

Bamboo worms

Bamboo worms, a type of moth larva, feed on flowering bamboo trees. They were originally collected straight from the trees, but are now raised on commercial farms, where they are also fed on organic vegetables and grains. When ready, the worms are quick-frozen.

The bamboo worm is a popular snack throughout Thailand, where it's known as *rot duan*, or 'express train', because of the speed at which it moves (which, given its popularity, is clearly not fast enough). In terms of taste and texture, the worms are similar to corn puffs; however, they're far more nutritious, being low in fat and high in protein and fibre. Uncooked worms are said to be mildly hallucinogenic.

SERVING SUGGESTION
Shallow-fry briefly in a wok, remove, and add a dash of Golden Mountain sauce and some Thai pepper powder. Enjoy with a cold beer.

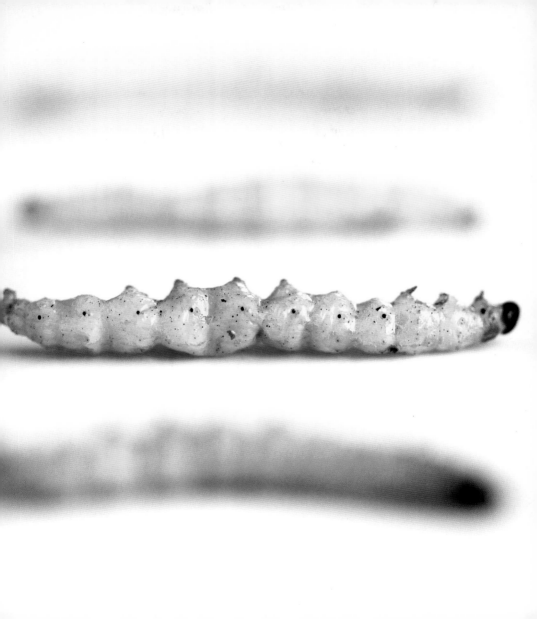

Bee cocoons on a stick

It probably takes far longer to prepare this particular
snack than it does to eat it: each individual cocoon is
threaded on to a stick before the whole lot is flash-fried.

SERVING SUGGESTION
Flash-fry in hot oil and season with salt, pepper and
spices. Alternatively, cook with soy sauce and sugar.

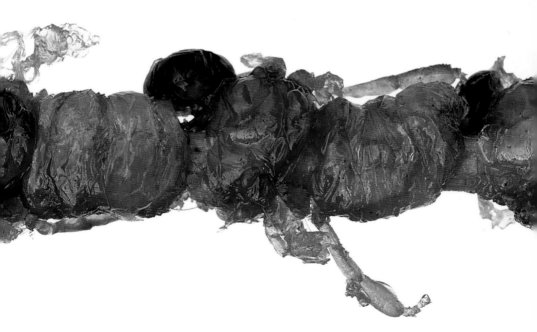

Black scorpion on a stick

'Warning: may contain poison' … Although the scorpion
is undoubtedly one of nature's survivors, a certain number
nevertheless end up for sale in the food markets of China
and Vietnam. In Beijing, black scorpion is regarded
as the 'lobster' of the species, and is correspondingly
more expensive than, for example, its yellow cousin
(see page 28). Eating black scorpion (crunchy on the
outside, and soft in the middle) is an experience you won't
forget in a hurry. Whether one should remove the sting
first is a matter of personal taste — and daring.

Dragonfly larvae on a stick

DONG HUA MEN NIGHT MARKET, BEIJING, CHINA

Centipede on a stick

25

Crickets

A delicacy throughout South-East Asia, deep-fried crickets — of the field variety — are especially popular in Thailand, where they are known as *jing leed*. In Bangkok, they are much sought-after by the girls and ladyboys working in the bars and clubs: during their breaks, they spill out into the *sois*, or alleys, of the city to buy a handful of the tasty critters. Humans are not alone in enjoying the insect nutritionally: live crickets are a favoured food source for such carnivorous pets as frogs, lizards and spiders.

SERVING SUGGESTION

Flash-fry in a wok. Remove, and add a light coating of Golden Mountain sauce and some Thai pepper powder.

Yellow scorpions on a stick

Before being fried alive, these fiesty snacks can be seen wriggling on the stick. At least you know they're fresh.

Dragonflies on a stick

Also known as 'sky prawns', dragonflies are eaten in both China and Indonesia.

Grub on a stick

The witchety grub, both raw and cooked, is well known as a staple food of the indigenous population of Australia. With a habit of burrowing into the roots of trees and bushes to feed off the wood and sap, it can be quite difficult to find. In China, deep-fried grubs are a little easier to obtain.

Long-horned beetles on a stick

As in the case of many of the stick-based foods in this book — prepared using long, kebab-style skewers — it takes considerable skill to rustle up long-horned beetles on a stick. The cook passes the stick through each insect with remarkable accuracy: put simply, it goes in one end and comes out the other.

Scorpion spirit

Scorpion spirit is sold throughout Asia in bottles of all shapes and sizes. As in the case of snake whisky (see page 180), it's usually drunk by businessmen as a sign of bravado. It's also believed to act as an aphrodisiac. For those wanting a little extra bite, the scorpion is sometimes joined by a snake – in a larger bottle.

Silkworm larvae on a stick

Silkworm larvae are eaten in many parts of Asia, including Cambodia, China, Laos, Thailand and Vietnam. In Korea, they are known as *beondegi*, and are sold from carts on the street; they can also be found — tinned — in supermarkets. High in protein, low in fat and an excellent source of essential amino acids, silkworm larvae have been proposed by Chinese researchers as the ideal food for astronauts on long-term missions into outer space. One small step for insect-kind?

Tarantula

In the West, the tarantula is a truly divisive creature. While many people regard it as the stuff of nightmares, others believe that it makes an ideal pet. In Cambodia, however, the locals just eat them. Sold on the street, especially at night, stir-fried tarantula is a very popular snack. It was also the inspiration behind the entire *Yuck!* project.

SERVING SUGGESTION

Strangle tarantula by pressing down firmly on its body. Remove and discard fangs, and wash spider thoroughly. Marinate for a while in some sugar and chilli oil. Heat a little oil in a wok and fry some garlic until crisp. Remove garlic and add spider. Stir-fry briefly with a dash of soy sauce. Warning: the belly may burst open at first bite, covering one's hand and face with black, pungent goo.

Weaver ants

Weaver ants take their name from their extraordinary nest-building behaviour. Working as a team, the ants construct their nests by weaving together leaves that are still attached to the host plant, using silk taken from their larvae. Colonies of weaver ants can be extremely large, often consisting of more than a hundred nests and more than half a million workers.

The ants and their eggs are consumed as a delicacy in north-eastern Thailand. Their slightly bitter taste means they are often used as flavouring in other dishes; however, they are also eaten raw or cooked with a small amount of seasoning. High in protein and low in fat, weaver ants are just one of the many wonder foods of the bug world – although their size makes them a relatively insubstantial snack.

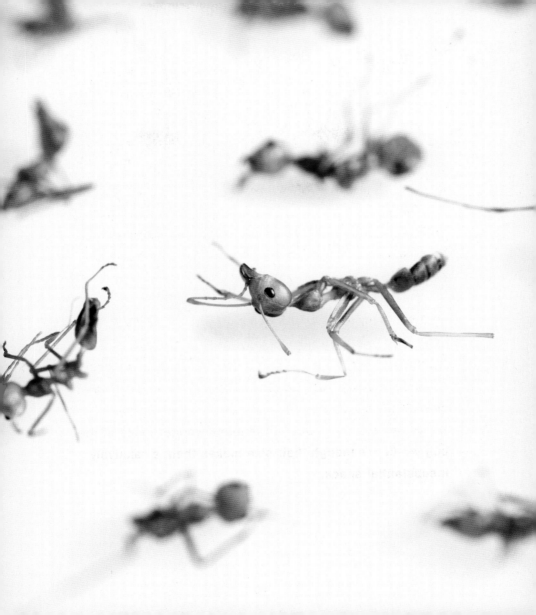

Worms

In Hanoi, whole buckets of slithering worms can be found at street markets, where they're sold by weight, alive. However, they're available for only one month in the autumn, when they surface to breed. While it's unlikely that you'd be served with a plate of wriggling worms, they are a key ingredient in other dishes.

SERVING SUGGESTION

Cover worms with boiling water, then chop and beat to form a thick paste. Mix paste with minced meat and a selection of chopped vegetables, herbs and seasoning. Form mixture into rissoles or burgers, and shallow-fry until cooked.

SEA MONSTERS

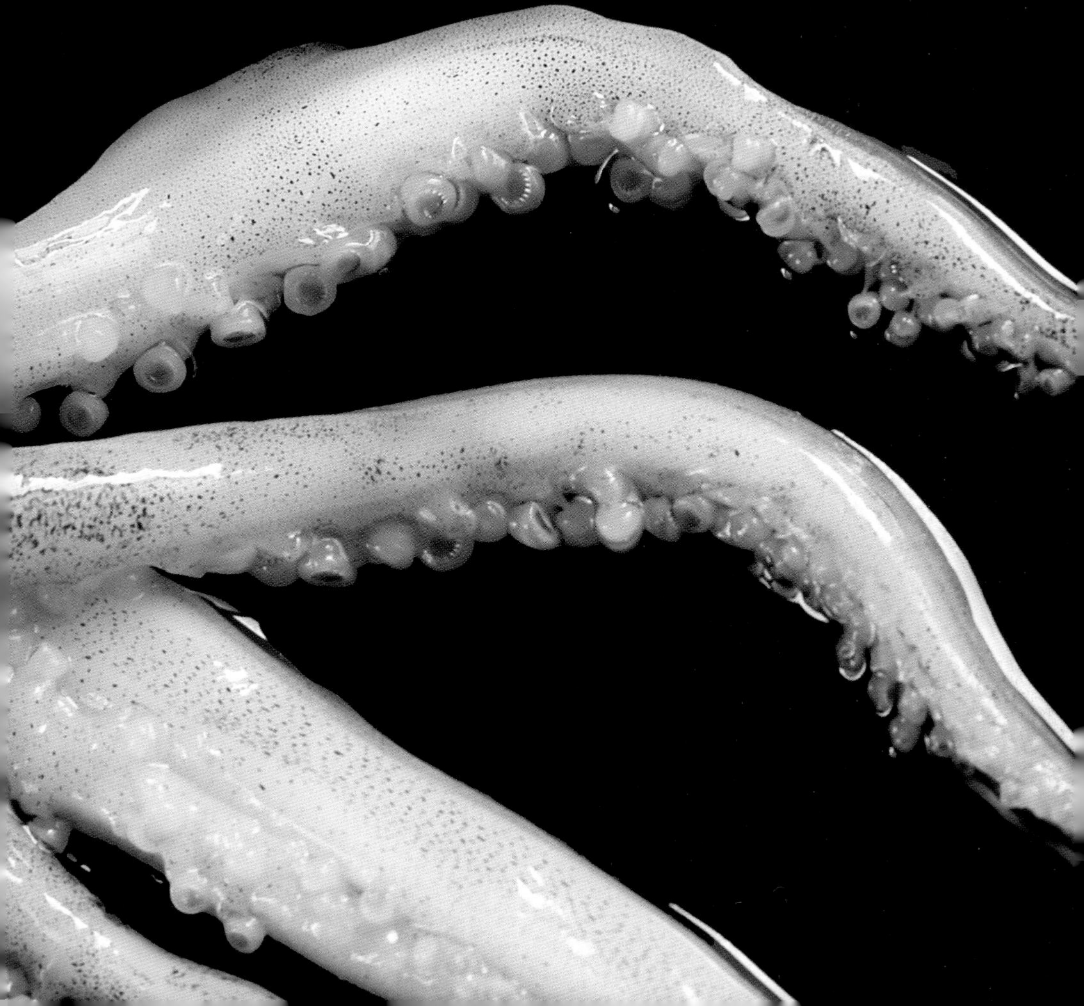

Abalone

The abalone, which can grow up to 20 cm (8 in.) in length, is an edible sea snail found in the coastal waters of almost every continent. In addition to having a rather risqué appearance, it's one of the most desired and expensive of all types of seafood. Consumed throughout Asia, abalones are especially popular in Japan, where they're eaten as sushi or *mizu gai*, a kind of sashimi. Elsewhere, the flesh is considered too tough to be eaten raw, and is tenderized before cooking. Abalones can also be bought dried or tinned.

Because abalones tend to reside at great depths, they are relatively difficult to obtain — and hence costly to buy. In Japan, they are historically caught by *ama*, female divers renowned for their ability to reach great depths without the use of breathing apparatus. Working in partnership with their husbands, the women wear special neoprene suits to prolong their dives.

Cod sperm

Fish sperm — in the form of milt, the male fish's semen-filled reproductive gland — is eaten worldwide (in some cases on toast). Even so, most consumers believe that they're eating roe rather than sperm. In Japan, where it's known as *shirako* (white children), milt is highly prized.

RECIPE

Steamed cod milt. Serves 2.

Ingredients: 120 ml (4$^1/_4$ fl oz) dashi; 2 tsp soy sauce; 1 tsp mirin; 30 g (1 oz) cod milt; a few sections of dried wakame seaweed; a pinch of thinly sliced spring onion.

Combine the dashi, soy sauce and mirin, and divide between two small bowls. Cut the milt in two, and place one half in each bowl. Add the seaweed, and garnish with onion if desired. Cover the bowls and steam for 5 to 7 minutes over a low heat, until the surface of the milt turns completely opaque and the ridges tighten and become more defined. Serve immediately.

Crabs on a stick

Starfish on a stick

Cuttlefish

Don't let the name fool you: the cuttlefish is in fact a type
of mollusc (as are the squid and the octopus) found in
the tropical and temperate waters of the world's oceans.
Most cuttlefish measure between 15 cm (6 in.) and
25 cm (10 in.) in length; in *The Oxford Companion to Food*
(1999), for example, the specimens referred to by Alan
Davidson are at the latter end of this scale. However, the
largest species can grow up to 50 cm (20 in.) long.

Although one is more likely to find squid (see page 86)
on a restaurant menu, cuttlefish is a particular favourite
in Italy, where it is used to make *risotto al nero di seppia*,
so-called because the cuttlefish's ink dyes the rice black.
In South-East Asia, dried, shredded cuttlefish is a popular
snack food. Nothing is wasted, however: the eyes are
often sold separately.

Eels

Eels are a popular dish in many parts of the world, from the United Kingdom, Italy and Sweden to China, Japan and South Korea. At Jagalchi Fish Market, the eels are prepared by the *azumas*, the brightly dressed women who look after the day-to-day running of the market. Famed for their tough exteriors, warm hearts and colourful rubber uniforms (aprons, gloves and wellies), the women secure the fish's head to a nail sticking out of a wooden block before stripping it of its skin (see page 13). The still-wriggling creature is then chucked into a plastic bowl, for sale.

The fish's popularity has raised some sustainability issues, however. In 2010 Greenpeace International added the European, Japanese and American eel to its seafood 'red list', which identifies those readily available fish that have a very high risk of being sourced from unsustainable fisheries.

Fish maw

One of the unexpected yet welcome consequences of compiling *Yuck!* has been the sudden increase in my knowledge of animal anatomy. Who knew, for example, that certain types of fish possess a 'maw', or swim bladder, an internal, gas-filled organ that allows the fish to regulate its buoyancy and depth in the water? What's more, who knew that many people like to eat it?

Sold by the sackload in markets, and in packets in shops, fish maw is a cheap treat throughout Asia and among Chinese communities worldwide; the dried variety is even sold by the Thai branch of a certain well-known British supermarket. Fish maw tends to be used as an ingredient in other dishes, especially soups and stews, giving the meal texture rather than a particularly strong flavour.

Squid eggs

There's a pleasing symmetry to finding such a small foodstuff in such an enormous venue. Open every Saturday and Sunday, Bangkok's Chatuchak Market is one of the world's greatest, containing more than 15,000 stalls selling everything from garden furniture and fashion to antiques and wildlife. Loved and loathed by tourists and locals alike, the market is an easy place in which to get lost, disorientated and, occasionally, ripped off. One of its saving graces, however, is its multitude of food stalls – including those selling fried squid eggs. Also known as 'octopus roe', the eggs are cooked in an enormous wok and served in plastic bowls with a sprinkling of salad and soy sauce to taste.

Geoduck clam

On the face of it, this revolting-looking specimen is the very epitome of *Yuck!*. The geoduck (pronounced 'gooeyduck') clam is the largest burrowing clam in the world, found in the mud, sand and gravel of the north-west coast of the United States and the west coast of Canada. Its hefty, meaty siphon, which can grow up to 100 cm (39 in.) long, is prized for its savoury flavour and crunchy texture. In China, the clam is eaten in a fondue-style hotpot; in Japan, it's consumed raw as sashimi. In Europe, though, it's relatively unknown.

Jellyfish

Yet another creature beleaguered by its reputation, this time as a danger to swimmers everywhere, the jellyfish is a popular foodstuff in many parts of the world, especially Asia. As in the case of fish maw (see page 57), it's often consumed as an ingredient in other dishes rather than as a snack or meal on its own. (With a wet, rubbery texture and little flavour to speak of, that's hardly surprising.) However, in China, for example, raw jellyfish is served shredded with a dressing of oil, soy sauce, rice vinegar and sugar; in Japan, the cured variety are rinsed, cut into strips and eaten with rice vinegar as an appetizer. Shredded jellyfish can also be added to salads: in *The Oxford Companion to Food*, Alan Davidson refers to *miang maeng kaphrung*, a Thai dish of jellyfish and green leaves.

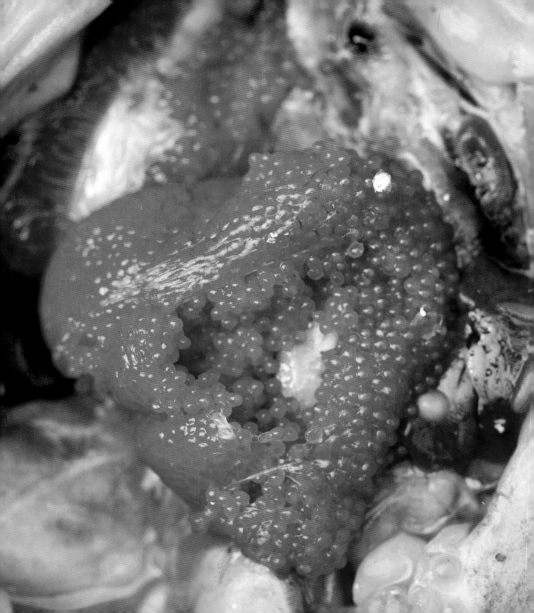

Monkfish roe

Not a natural beauty, the monkfish nevertheless contains something rather wonderful within. While its tail is a menu regular in restaurants worldwide, it's the fish's tomato-red roe — seen here on display at a market in Seoul — that make it truly special. The roe may be eaten raw, fried or as a soup; the fish's liver is also a hidden treat.

Octopus

From this angle, the octopus makes a disturbing sight, its mouth looming ominously at the top of an array of sucker-clad tentacles. Indeed, the 'devil-fish' (as it's known by divers in the United States) has often been portrayed as a monster of the deep — not least in certain disaster movies of the 1970s. But despite this bad press, it's also a favourite of seafood enthusiasts worldwide.

Like its cousin the squid (see page 86), the octopus is at its best when fresh, and at its worst when overcooked. Baby octopus need no preparation, but larger models require serious tenderizing, the various methods of which have almost become folklore. In Japan, where it's known as *tako*, octopus is a key ingredient in sushi; it's also a staple of Mediterranean cooking. In Korea, they take the 'fresh is best' mantra very seriously indeed: the octopus's legs are sometimes sliced from the live animal and eaten while they're still moving.

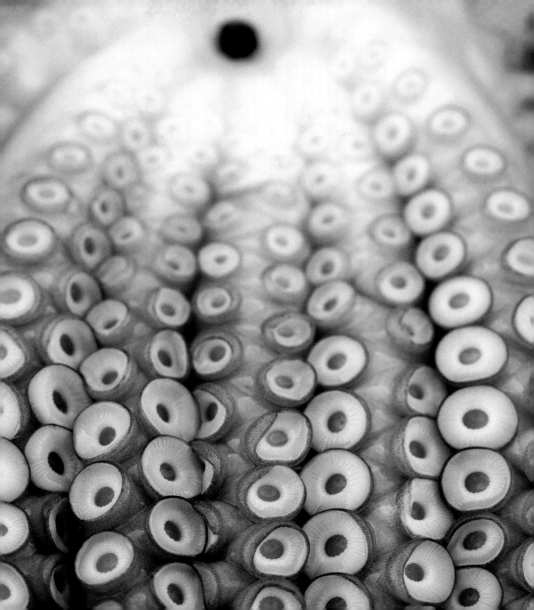

Ray

In South Korea, rays — often called skate in the United Kingdom — can be bought either fresh or dried. To keep the fish spread out while drying, the vendors 'thread' its wings with chopsticks, which act rather like splints (see below). In culinary terms, the most prized parts of the ray are its wings (usually eaten dried), its 'cheeks' (the area surrounding the eyes) and its liver; the rest of the fish is considered too rubbery to be of any value. Ray dishes can be simple or sophisticated, as in the case of *raie au beurre noir* (ray with black butter). Recipes for stingrays are plentiful: in Singapore and Malaysia, for example, barbecued stingray served with spicy sambal sauce is a particular favourite.

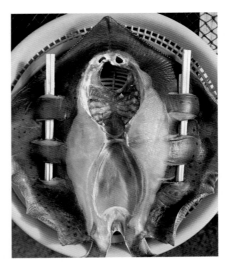

Razor clams

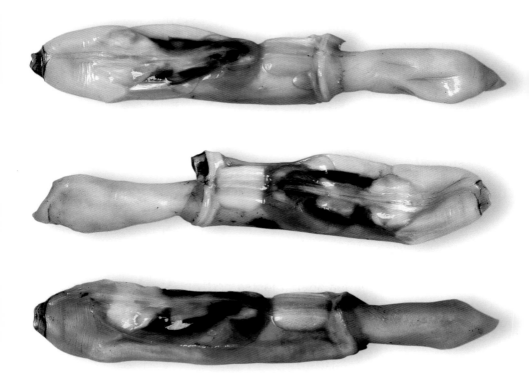

JAGALCHI FISH MARKET, BUSAN, SOUTH KOREA

Sea cucumber

If I had to rank the various foods in this book by, well, yuckiness, then the sea cucumber would be a close contender for the top spot. It tastes pretty much as it looks: wet, slimy, slug-ish, vaguely metallic and gelatinous. And did I mention chewy? In China, where it's often sold in dried form, the sea cucumber is eaten as much for its perceived health benefits as its taste.

Salamander on a stick

In Beijing, this snack is also known as 'sea dog'.

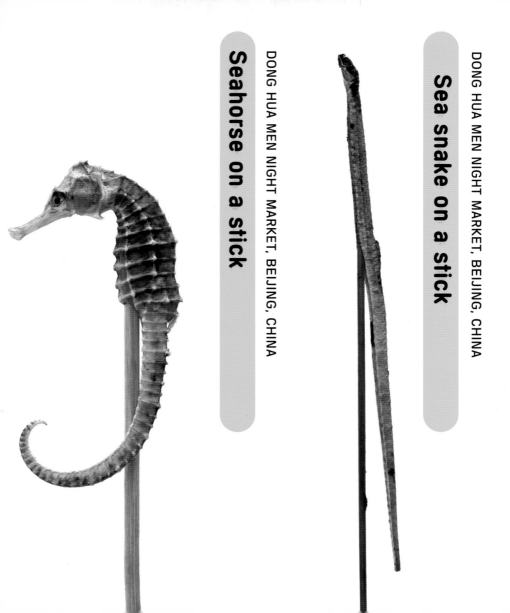

DONG HUA MEN NIGHT MARKET, BEIJING, CHINA

Sea snake on a stick

DONG HUA MEN NIGHT MARKET, BEIJING, CHINA

Seahorse on a stick

Sea squirt

The sea squirt is an unusual type of marine animal that falls in the grey area between invertebrates and vertebrates. It spends its days in shallow waters, firmly attached to a rock or shell, and feeds by filtering sea water through two slits in its body, which can grow up to 15 cm (6 in.) in length. It gets its name from its tendency, when handled, to spray its unsuspecting captor with water.

The best way to get at the yellow flesh inside the sea squirt is to split it in half, like a sea urchin (see overleaf). However, with a flavour not unlike iodine, it may not be to everyone's taste. Also known as *figue de mer* (sea fig), the animal is consumed primarily in Korea and, to a lesser extent, Japan, where it is eaten raw as sashimi. It can also be salted, dried, smoked, grilled or deep-fried.

Sea urchin

The edible parts of this hedgehog of the sea are its ovaries, also known as 'corals' or 'roe' – a delicious cross between seafood and fruit. They can be eaten raw, or used for sauces, soups, omelettes and soufflés.

Korean penis fish

Looking like extras from a David Cronenberg movie, these phallic monstrosities are probably one of the last things you'd want to see on your dinner plate. Not so in South Korea, where the locals regularly tuck into them with relish. To give the creature its Latin (and, by comparison, rather dull) name, *Urechis unicinctus* is in fact a type of spoon worm, a marine animal that lives in burrows or crevices in shallow water.

While the penis fish is particularly popular in Korea, where it's known as *gaebul* and sold alive in huge tanks of water, it can also be found in the fish markets of China and Japan.

Seaweed

It may not have the shock factor of, say, the Korean penis fish (see page 78), but, to some, seaweed is just as yucky. Essentially a sea vegetable, seaweed is eaten almost anywhere with a coastline. It's also very good for you, being high in iron and low in fat, as well as a good source of protein and some key vitamins and minerals. While tinned and powdered varieties are available, they're not nearly as good as the fresh stuff.

How seaweed is eaten depends very much on geography. In Japan, for example, it's used to wrap rice in sushi; in Korea, it's sometimes roasted using sesame oil. In Wales, cooked seaweed is known as laverbread, and can be found in the markets of the south coast. Traditionally, it's mixed with oatmeal, formed into small patties, fried and served with bacon and cockles. However, it's also eaten grilled, on toast — which is how I prefer it.

Shark

Demand for shark meat is booming, from the dogfish to the enormous whale shark. Indeed, it's now possible to buy the white, boneless flesh in supermarkets in Europe, the United States and South America. Unfortunately, this is putting some species under threat (see also overleaf). While small or baby sharks are often sold whole, shark meat is most popular in steak form. In Iceland, preparation

of the meat is a long, involved process. To make *hákarl*, or 'fermented shark' – a traditional Icelandic dish made from either Greenland or basking shark – the fish's carcass is cured for six to twelve weeks, cut into strips and then dried for several months. Although historically eaten as part of the country's midwinter festivities, it's readily available all year round. Extremely fishy in flavour, *hákarl* has an unforgettable, amonia-rich smell, strong enough to knock your (probably less pongy) socks off.

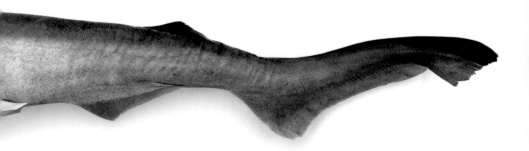

Shark's fin

In Bangkok's Chinatown, shark's fin restaurants abound, with shark's fin soup at the top of the menu; it's also sold frozen in many Asian supermarkets. Reputed to have aphrodisiacal qualities, the soup is made using chicken broth, with the fins giving it a gelatinous quality. In terms of flavour, it doesn't really taste of a great deal, not least shark itself: you either love it or loathe it. Nor does it come cheap, its high price confirming it as a high-status dish.

Sadly, the soup's perceived exclusivity has had a detrimental effect on populations of the one hundred or so species deliberately targeted for their fins. What's more, as the fins become harder to come by through overfishing, the dish is seen as even more desirable, and so demand increases further. To compound the situation, the sharks are sometimes caught solely for their fins, with the rest of the fish going to waste.

Squid

While the giant version remains largely the stuff of myth and legend — tantalizingly beyond the reach of most efforts to document it — the smaller, edible species is a common fixture on restaurant menus worldwide. The animal, which is usually no more than 60 cm (24 in.) long, may be eaten in a wide variety of styles, including raw, grilled, stewed and, of course, fried. As in the case of the cuttlefish (see page 52), its ink also has culinary uses, as an addition to such dishes as risotto, soup and pasta. Baby squid are sometimes eaten live, although the risk of the creature's suckers attaching themselves to one's tongue may put off some people.

Turtle

Today, turtle flesh is mostly consumed in parts
of Asia, where it is considered a delicacy. For
many years, however, it was also a staple of Anglo-
American cuisine. Indeed, a recipe for turtle soup
can be found in *The Household Cyclopedia of General
Information*, a guide to housekeeping published in the
United States in 1881. (The recipe calls for a 'fine, lively,
fat turtle'.) In fact, the dish is still popular in some
southern states of the country. In the United Kingdom,
Queen Victoria and Prince Albert were said to begin their
Christmas dinner with turtle soup.

In Hanoi, turtles are sold at street markets. As in the
case of many of the animals in this section of the book,
however, demand for turtle meat has put some species
under threat. Although wild turtles continue to be caught
and sold in large numbers, efforts are now being made
to meet demand using farm-raised animals.

Whelk

In certain parts of the United Kingdom, the whelk — or sea snail, a large marine mollusc — is the quintessential seaside snack, usually doused in malt vinegar and sprinkled with a little salt. It's also a popular foodstuff in large parts of Asia, including Taiwan, South Korea and Japan. Particularly large varieties occur in the United States and Canada, where they're chopped and tinned, or packed into jars with sugar and spiced vinegar. Whelks of all types can be grilled, steamed or boiled, but they become rubbery if overcooked. The animal's smaller brother, the winkle, is the main ingredient in another traditional seaside 'treat': the winkle sandwich.

THE WHOLE HOG

Dog

How much is that doggy in the window? In the West, eating man's best friend is widely regarded as unconscionable. Not so in Vietnam, China and South Korea, where dog is a popular dish. In Hanoi, for example, a whole area of the city specializes in dog-meat restaurants.

In some Asian communities, dog is said to bring good luck when consumed at certain times of the lunar month. It's also eaten almost exclusively by businessmen — as part of a kind of alpha-male ritual — in the belief that the meat will make them virile. At the very least, dog is extremely versatile: while in Beijing, I came across a recipe book outlining 167 different ways to cook the animal.

Blood sausage

Despite being taboo to many people, eating blood is a truly international phenomenon — not least in the form of a sausage. In Peru, blood sausage is called *relleno*; elsewhere, it's known as black pudding (United Kingdom) and *boudin noir* (France). Wherever it's eaten, and whatever it's called, the dish is basically a blend of animal blood (usually a pig's) and one or more 'fillers', such as pork fat, bread, onion, barley or oatmeal.

If eating blood sausage isn't your thing, then you can always throw it. At the World Black Pudding Throwing Championship, held each year in Manchester, England, the winner is the contestant who dislodges the most number of Yorkshire puddings from a ledge using 170-g (6-oz) sections of the local blood sausage. The contest is said to be rooted in an incident from the War of the Roses, when, according to legend, both sides resorted to throwing food at each other after running out of ammunition.

Camel jerky

It may look like something you might find down the back of the sofa, but camel jerky — made from Australia's burgeoning feral camel population — is a great alternative to the beef version.

Curried dog on a stick

99

Cow's cheek

Recipes for cow's, or beef, cheek can be found in cookery books worldwide. The most traditional way of cooking beef cheek, however, is to braise it. Patience is an essential ingredient: hours of cooking are required to ensure that the meat is tender when eaten.

SERVING SUGGESTION

Sauté some onion, carrots, celery and garlic in olive oil, adding generous pinches of rosemary and thyme. Place the sautéd ingredients in some beef stock, stir thoroughly, and add the beef cheek. Braise for at least three or four hours, or until tender. Serve beef and stock together.

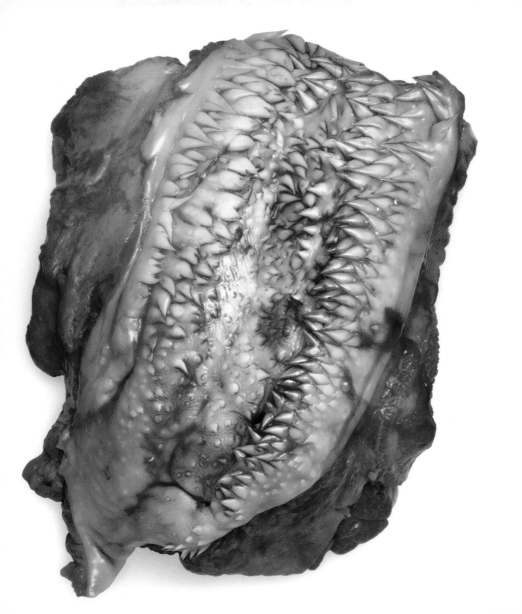

EAST STREET MARKET, WALWORTH, LONDON

Cow's face

Cow's skin (including the face), or *pomo*, is a speciality of Nigerian cooking.

Cow's feet

Putting a foot in one's mouth is usually a faux pas. Not so in Africa, where cow's-feet soup or stew is enjoyed by many.

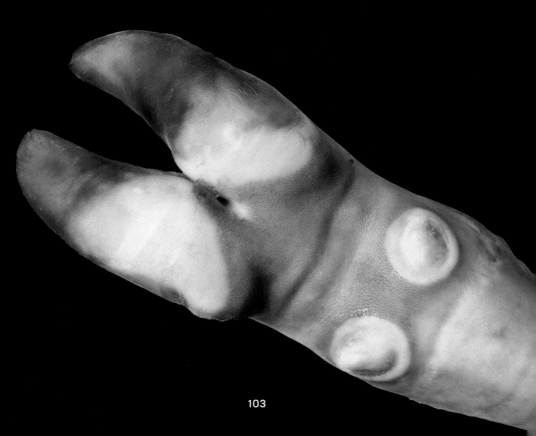

Goat's testicles

The idea of eating testicles of any kind is likely to bring tears to the eyes of large numbers of the male population. However, the wide consumption of goat's testicles throughout Africa and Indonesia is a good example of man's resourceful use of every part of an animal for nutritional benefit.

Interestingly, many cuisines shy away from the word 'testicles', preferring instead to use more palatable euphemisms; in the United States, for example, lamb's testicles are known as 'fries', while those of a bull are referred to as 'Rocky Mountain oysters'. In the Middle East, testicles are often served as part of a mezze.

SERVING SUGGESTION

Remove the outer membrane, and cut testicles into cubes. Marinate in a mix of lemon juice and soy sauce before chargrilling on skewers.

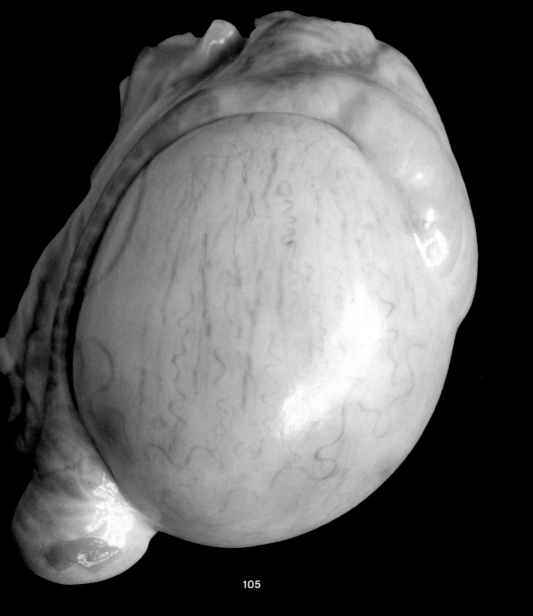

Donkey

High in protein and low in fat, donkey meat is a speciality in both France and China. The French, who are also partial to horse, enjoy it as *saucisson d'âne* (donkey sausage). In China, meanwhile, ready-cooked donkey meat is sold in vacuum packs (see below). To quote the shakily translated blurb from the back of one such pack, donkey meat 'is the best goods for present, banquet and trip'. Indeed!

Goat's head

Goat's head is enjoyed in parts of Africa, India, Europe and the Caribbean. In India, it's used to make the self-explanatory goat's-head curry. *Isi ewu*, or spiced goat's head, is a very popular dish from eastern Nigeria, usually prepared with enough chillis to remove one's own cranium. The eyeballs are served to the guest of honour.

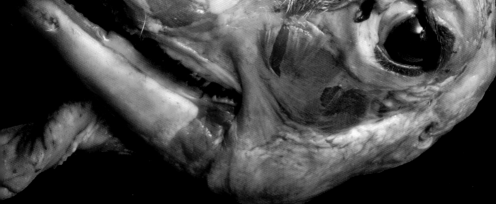

Goat's feet

Like those of the cow (see page 103) and lamb, goat's
feet are often used as the basis for soups and stews.
Popular in Africa and Indonesia, among other countries.

Guinea pig

Roast guinea pig, or *cuy*, is a dish native to Peru. The animal varies hugely in size, and is ordered by weight or portion. You're never quite sure how it will appear on your plate, though, and it took me about five orders to get this particular specimen: served whole —

spatchcocked — on

a bed of potatoes with

a spicy tomato sauce.

Hare

Recipes for hare appear as early as the eighteenth century. Although less popular now, it was once eaten widely in the United Kingdom, France and Germany. Today, hare is mainly used for stews and casseroles; in Belgium, it's cooked with beer, chestnuts and prunes. Jugged hare – 'jugging' being the process of stewing game meat in a casserole – is the ultimate classic country dish; the animal's blood is used for the gravy.

Pig's head

This is one of my favourite foods. While the ears, nose and cheeks may be prime cuts for some, the whole head can be deconstructed into jellied brawn. Known also as 'head cheese', *fromage de tête* (France) and *coppa di testa* (Italy), brawn is mostly eaten in Europe, although variations can be found in Asia and the Middle East. Historically, it was made using the head of a wild boar.

SERVING SUGGESTION

Place a cleaned pig's head, together with the animal's trotters and tail, in a large saucepan of boiling water. Simmer for 24 hours, then leave to cool. Drain off and reserve the stock, and remove the meat from the head. Chop all the meat finely, and transfer to a bowl. Add some chopped fennel and some sliced carrots and shallots. Stir in some thyme and sage, season with celery salt, and mix everything together. Spoon the mixture into a serving dish, sprinkle with lemon juice, and cover with the stock. Refrigerate until set.

Kangaroo tail

Kangaroo meat was once eaten only by the indigenous population of Australia. As a 'bush food', it was an important source of nutrition for the Aborigines; a single animal would be shared between many. Today, it's available worldwide, especially from the 'exotic meat' sections of farmers' markets; at London's Borough Market, for example, it's sold as burgers or steak alongside zebra, ostrich and antelope meat. In Australia, one can still eat kangaroo tail as part of an authentic 'outback' experience.

In a re-creation of the traditional method of cooking the animal practised by the Arrernte people of central and northern Australia, the tails are first of all singed to remove the hair (see right). They are then buried in the ground with hot coals, and dug up again once cooked. The meat itself is very low in both fat and cholesterol.

Sheep's tongue

As English artist, writer, musician and all-round wit Vivian Stanshall once said, 'I wouldn't eat anything that's been in someone else's mouth.' But sheep's tongue is truly delicious; in the form of terrine, it's particularly popular in the Middle East and the Caribbean. To make them tender, tongues in general require prolonged moist cooking, which often takes the form of braising.

Bushman's platter

This selection of cold meats (clockwise from right: kangaroo, emu and camel) began life as a dish aimed firmly at the tourist. Recently, what might be called the 'Aussie ploughmans' has become equally popular with the resident population. The Australian government is particularly keen to promote its consumption as part of a healthy lifestyle: all three meats are low in cholesterol.

Ox tongue

Along with sheep's tongue (see page 118) — and, indeed, offal in general — ox tongue has recently received the renewed attention of a number of noted English chefs, including Fergus Henderson and Hugh Fearnley-Whittingstall. Such expert reappraisal has elevated what many people still regard as a base product into the realms of fine dining. Further afield, ox tongue is widely used in the cuisines of such countries as Mexico, Russia, the Philippines and Japan.

Ox heart

Pig's brain

When most people talk about 'brain food', this is probably not what they have in mind. But in the Philippines, for example, pig's brain forms the basis of a number of popular dishes, including *tortang utak* (pig's brain omelette; see below). Also popular in China, Europe and other parts of South-East Asia.

SERVING SUGGESTION
Scoop out the brains from a pig's head. Boil, and divide in half, as though splitting a bread roll. Dip each half in beaten eggs, and fry.

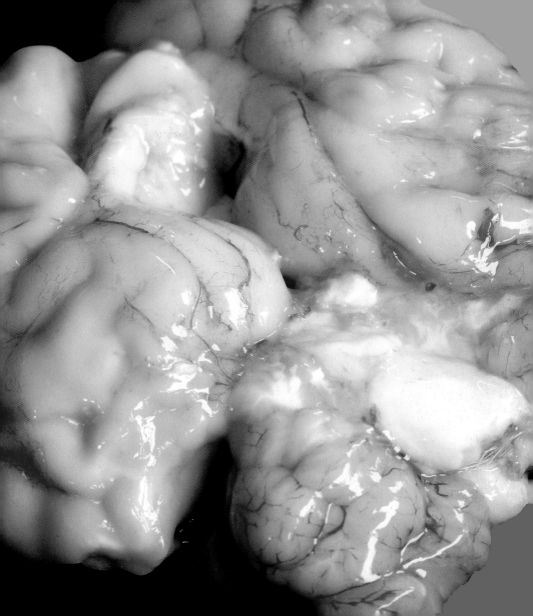

Pig's face

To fully appreciate the remarkable colour and texture
of this juicy creation, one really has to get up close and
personal. Barbecued pig's face is a Chinese speciality,
eaten throughout the country itself and where there
are large Chinese communities, such as in Bangkok.
It's usually sold hot, in strips, in a bag — like a kind
of pig jerky.

In addition to being barbecued, pig's face is often used as
an ingredient in other recipes. It can also form the basis
of an unusual cold cut, 'cured rolled face', but patience is
a must: preparation of the dish, which involves curing and
cooking the meat very slowly, takes up to nine days.

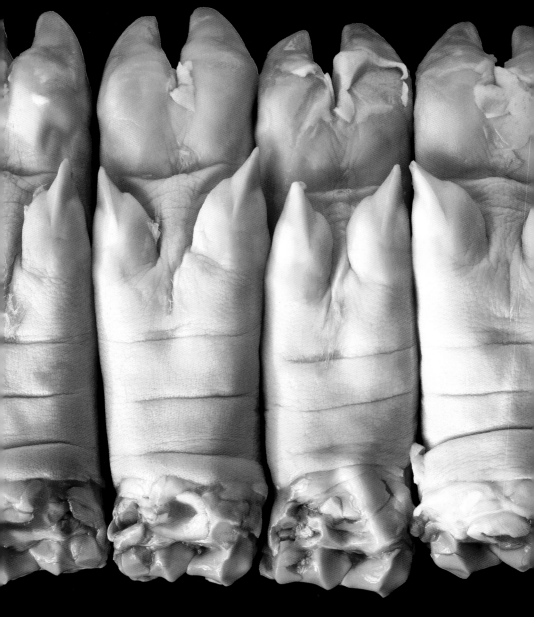

Pig's trotters

When it comes to eating them, pig's trotters — or, to dispense with the euphemism, pig's feet — are a remarkably versatile part of the animal, a favourite of the 'waste not, want not' school of cookery. They can be roasted, pickled, stuffed, baked, deep-fried, caramelized or made into a terrine (which requires hours and hours of boiling to separate the soft tissue). In Korea, they form the key ingredient in *jokbal*, boiled pig's feet flavoured with leeks, garlic, ginger, rice wine, sugar and soy sauce. *Jokbal* is considered an *anju*, or side dish, and is eaten with alcohol and served with other *anjus*, to be shared with friends. It takes time to prepare, but perhaps that's what makes it special.

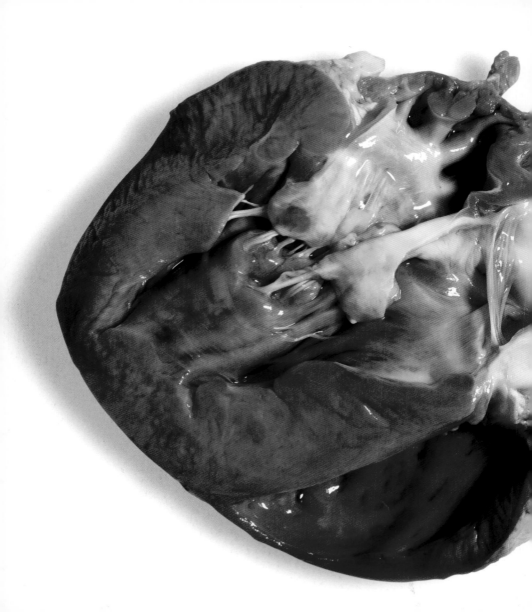

Pig's heart

Delicious, nutritious, but maybe not for the faint-hearted (sorry), pig's hearts can be grilled, braised, roasted or stewed. For obvious reasons, they won't look like this on your plate.

Pig's large intestine

Photographing the large intestine of a pig was no picnic:
in terms of both sight and smell, it's a truly 'Yuck!' food.
Eaten in Asia, Europe and the United States.

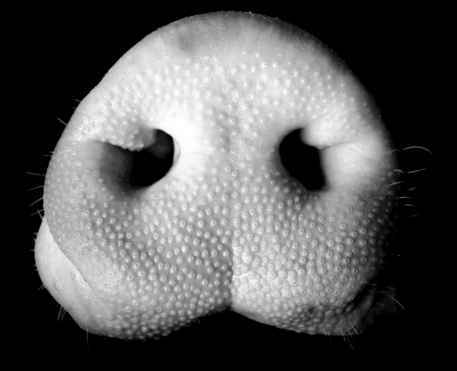

CENTRAL MARKET, CARDIFF

Pig's snout

An international foodstuff, pig's snout is a key ingredient
in *sisig*, a spicy Filippino dish made from fried pig's snout
and ears. It's also the icon of the 'nose to tail' school of
eating, founded by Fergus Henderson.

Chitterlings

Chitterlings, the intestines of a pig prepared as food, can be found in most pork-eating cultures. In the United States, where they're known as 'chitlins', they form an important part of the cuisine and culture of the Deep South. In Salley, South Carolina (population 410), the annual 'Chitlin Strut!' festival attracts some 25,000 visitors each year. There's even a song devoted to the foodstuff, 'Chitlin Cookin' Time in Cheatham County', in which the singer states, rather mournfully, 'I've a longin' that the chitlins will fill'.

The preparation of raw chitterlings requires nothing if not dedication. In particular, it's vital that they're cleaned thoroughly, by hand, before being cooked. And, as in the case of all offal, the fresher the better.

Pig's spleen

Although pig's spleen is used by cooks as far afield as China, South-East Asia and Belgium, it is perhaps in Sicily where the foodstuff has come into its own. *Pane con la milza*, essentially a spleen sandwich, is unique to this autonomous region of Italy, in particular the area around Palermo. The meat is cut into strips, deep-fried and then served in a bread roll with a slice of fresh Sicilian lemon and some grated local caciocavallo cheese.

Pig's tail

Used in soup and for stock, roast pig's tail is a popular foodstuff in many Asian communities.

Pig's stomach

Although pig's stomach, or maw, is commonly used as an ingredient in Asian cooking, its origins as a foodstuff can be traced back to eighteenth-century Germany. There, it was used by farmers to make *Saumagen*, pan-fried or roasted pig's stomach stuffed with pork, vegetables, herbs and spices. The dish, created to make use of leftovers, accompanied German immigrants on their journey to the New World; today, Americans refer to it as stuffed hog maw.

SERVING SUGGESTION

Mix together some chopped onions and carrots, diced potatoes and sausage meat, and season. Stuff mixture into a pig's stomach, and secure with a skewer. Place stomach in a roasting dish with a little water, cover, and bake at a high temperature for approximately three hours. Remove the lid for the last half hour of cooking to brown the meat.

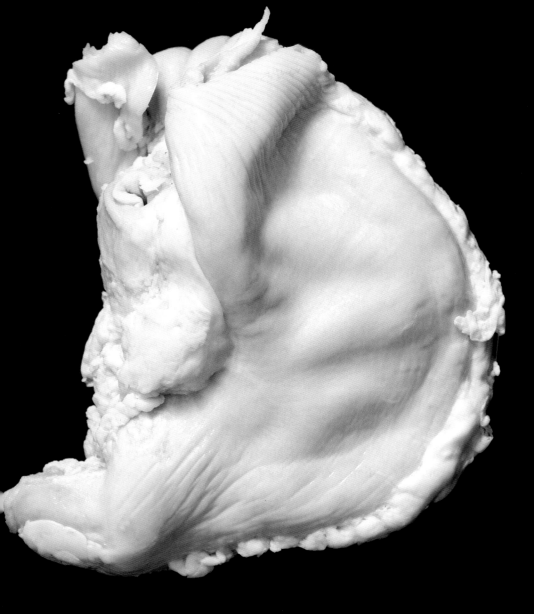

Pig's tongue with gullet

Looking more like something from a biology lesson than kitchen fare, pig's tongue differs only slightly from the sheep and ox varieties (see pages 118 and 122 respectively): it's sold with the gullet still attached. Eaten worldwide, pig's tongue can be used in stews, or braised in cider with pigs' cheeks.

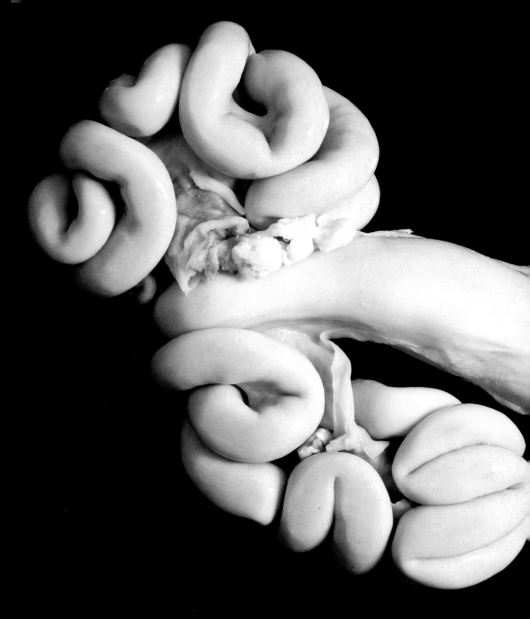

Pig's uterus

Not having been to medical school, I had to rely on the English translation on this foodstuff's packaging to tell me exactly what it was. Smelling a little like a very wet dog, pig's uterus is often stuffed with other ingredients — including minced pork, vegetables and spices — before being cooked. Popular throughout Asia, especially China and the Philippines.

Rabbit

Despite the 'eating one's childhood pet' overtones, rabbit remains one of my favourite foods. Full of flavour, high in protein and low in fat, it's consumed in many parts of the world, especially Europe and South America. In Malta, rabbit is practically the national dish, and is eaten with pasta, in traditional stews or as fine cuisine, often with prunes. The meat of the female rabbit (doe) is considered superior to that of the male (buck).

Rat

Together with spiders and dogs, rats figure highly on most people's lists of things they would never, ever consider eating. This smoked specimen was one of a pair that I bought from an old lady sitting at the side of the road in Vientiane, Laos. When I began to negotiate over the price, she looked at me like it was the most natural thing in the world. And no, I didn't eat them.

Rats are consumed throughout South-East Asia. They're also eaten in north-east India, in the state of Bihar: there, the Musahar community — traditional eaters of field rats — now farm the animals on a commercial basis. Before you make a beeline for your nearest sewer, however, it's probably worth bearing in mind that field rats tend to have a much healthier diet than their urban cousins.

Sheep's head

It's hard to deny the purely visceral impact of this particular item. In culinary terms, sheep's head is eaten in many parts of the world, from Asia, Africa and the Middle East to Iceland and Scandinavia. In Norway, the residents of Voss, a small town in the south-west of the country, are very keen on *smalahove*, or smoked sheep's head. Only the bones remain uneaten: as in the case of goat's head (see page 108), the eyes are regarded as the highlight of the dish.

Sheep's heart

Sheep's heart — roasted and stuffed — made a regular
appearance on my dinner plate when I was growing up,
and it remains a firm favourite. As in the case of all offal,
it does not keep well and must be cooked while still fresh.

RECIPE

Stuffed sheep's hearts. Serves 4–5.
2 sheep's hearts; 1 small onion, chopped; 1 rasher of
bacon, chopped; 4 tbsp breadcrumbs; 1 tbsp chopped
suet; a little stock; 1 tsp parsley, chopped; grated rind
of $\frac{1}{2}$ lemon; 1 egg, beaten.

Wash the hearts and cut away any veins or gristle. Lightly
sauté the onion and bacon, add the rest of the ingredients,
and bind everything together with the beaten egg. Stuff
the mixture into the hearts, and sew them up. Place the
hearts in a baking tin with a little stock, and bake at a
moderate temperature (180° C/360° F) for about two
hours, basting often. Serve with gravy and redcurrant jelly.

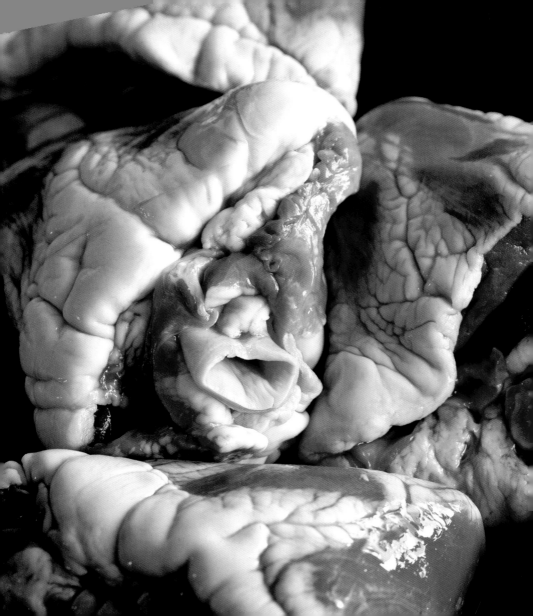

DONG HUA MEN NIGHT MARKET, BEIJING, CHINA

Sheep's penis on a stick

Although the cooking process may lessen the impact of this self-explanatory snack (the raw version is shown opposite), it's not the size that matters but what you do with it that counts – as in so much in life. What the Chinese do with it, of course, is eat it.

EAST STREET MARKET, WALWORTH, LONDON

Tripe

It's all in the name. Some people use the word 'tripe' as slang for something that's false, worthless or rubbish. For me, it will always refer to my favourite childhood dish bar none. Essentially part of the stomach of a cow, tripe can also be made from the gut of an ox, sheep, goat or pig. Beef tripe is usually made from only the first three chambers of a cow's stomach (it has four); the aptly named honeycomb tripe, shown here, is made using the reticulum, or second chamber. In my experience, the people who express the most vehement opinions against tripe are the ones who've never actually tried it.

SERVING SUGGESTION

Poach tripe in milk, with onions and a bay leaf, until tender. Serve with mashed potatoes.

SNAKES ON A PLATE

Barbecued river frogs

Battered frogs

Crocodile jerky

Another exotic alternative to the beef variety, crocodile jerky is also enjoyed in South Africa and China.

Deep-fried river frogs

Reminiscent of both the bodies at Pompeii and the members of a ballet troupe, these crispy little beauties are a popular snack throughout South-East Asia.

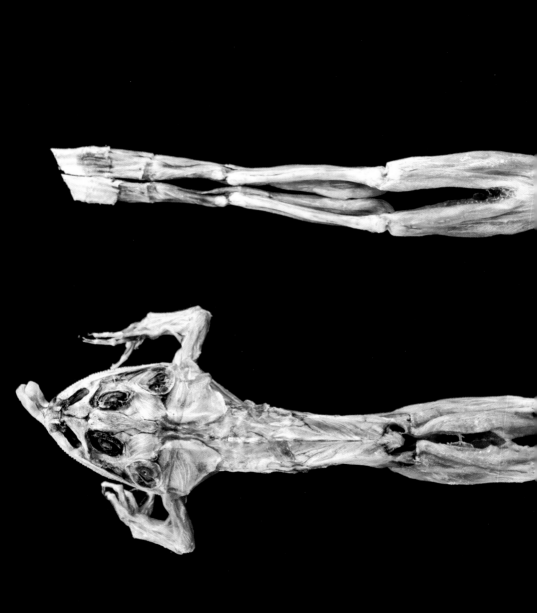

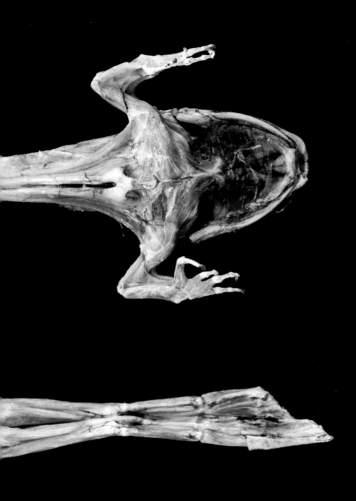

Dried frogs

While they wouldn't look out of place in a sci-fi movie, dried frogs are actually used to make soup.

PHNOM PENH, CAMBODIA

Dried river snake

Used in the preparation of soup, these richly coloured specimens are best described as coiled Cambodian stock cubes.

Snake on a stick

There's not much more to be said, really: you get what you pay for.

Frog porridge

Not perhaps what we in the West would regard as traditional breakfast fare, frog porridge (or congee) is very popular in parts of Sout-East Asia. So much so that restaurants there have named themselves after the dish. At one of the many Eminent Frog Porridge restaurants in Singapore, I was caught by a tropical rainstorm while photographing a bowl of the foodstuff on a terrace. In a manner that is typical of the 'can do' attitude of the region, the entire staff – without saying a word – rushed outside, picked up my table, the porridge and my entire makeshift photo studio, and carried it all indoors. Before I could even say thank you, they returned seamlessly to their work.

Frog porridge is usually served with spring onions and chilli sauce. Each serving is priced according to the number of legs desired: two, four, six, eight and so on. While the frog meat is so tender that it falls off the bone, the porridge element is an acquired taste.

Frogs' legs

This long-established staple of French cuisine is these days eaten far more widely, in Asia, the Americas and other parts of Europe. As Alan Davidson notes in *The Oxford Companion to Food*, many of the frogs' legs consumed in France come from outside the country. For many years the chief exporter was India, but the trade was banned after it became clear that shrinking frog populations meant less effective insect control. Today, frozen frogs' legs may reach Europe from as far afield as Japan.

In Asian markets, frog-selling is a two-man operation. One vendor, wielding a machete, decapitates and skins (see page 10), while the other bags and sells. The drama doesn't end there, however: the legs continue to twitch and stretch for some time after they've been separated from the rest of the body, shocking the unprepared shopper and still-life photographer in equal measure.

Dried lizard

While chicken soup is a traditional 'get well' dish in the West, the Chinese like to take things a little bit further – by using dried lizards instead. Found in Chinese medicine shops throughout Asia, the lizards are often sold in pairs: one male and one female. For best results, it's said that both lizards should be 'cooked' together.

Snake pancake rolls

The restaurants in the village of Le Mat, on the outskirts of Hanoi, specialize in just one ingredient: the snake. Abundant supplies from nearby snake farms have enabled enterprising local chefs to conjure up creative menus from this one, hissing life form, celebrated each year at the Le Mat Snake Festival. Diners can enjoy snake-wine aperitifs, snake cakes, crispy snakeskin, barbecued snake and, of course, snake pancake rolls. Surrounding them are huge jars containing coiled snakes in alcoholic spirit. Given the richness of the animal's meat, a shot of this 'snake whisky' (see overleaf) is recommended as a digestif.

Snake whisky

Snake whisky — in bottles of all shapes and sizes — can be found in shops and eating establishments throughout Asia, from tiny market stalls to high-end restaurants and bars. Wherever it's sold, the sales pitch is always the same: 'Make you strong, sir! Make you strong!' Whether this claim has any basis in truth remains open to debate, but the product's continued existence and continuing sales suggest that someone, somewhere, still believes. If snake preserved in alcohol doesn't appeal, then the scorpion variety (see page 34) might be your thing.

Snakeskin on a stick

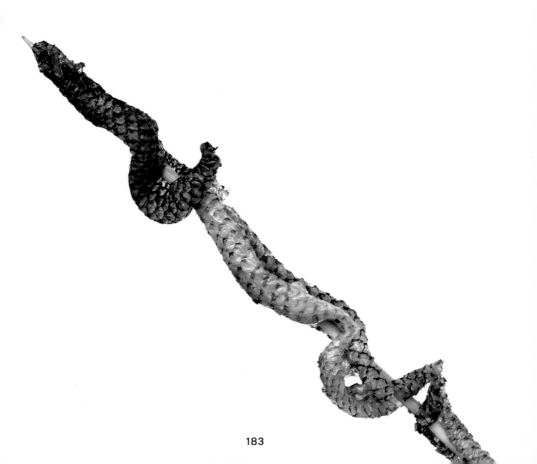

BIRDS OF A FEATHER

Black-skinned chicken

You couldn't make it up. The silkie, as it's more commonly known, is one unique breed of chicken. Named for its fluffy, silky plumage (available in a range of colours), it's also known for its blue earlobes; for having five toes on each foot rather than the usual four; and, of course, for its extraordinary blue-black skin. A very docile, easy-going animal, it's often exhibited at poultry shows.

As food, the silkie is highly valued throughout Asia, especially for its deep, gamey flavour. In China, for example, where it's also prized for its medicinal properties, the bird is most commonly used to make soup. Elsewhere in the region, it's sometimes braised or made into a curry. Although most Western cuisines have long shunned the silkie, demand is on the increase among growing Asian communities in such countries as the United States.

Raw blood soup

The word alone is enough to deter many people, especially when uttered in the same sentence as 'food preparation', but blood in varying forms has been used as an ingredient throughout history. Usually, however, its use is a little less blatant than in *tiet canh*, or blood soup, a traditional Vietnamese dish made using the blood of a duck. Sold from market stalls selling every other bit of the animal, the soup is eaten very, very fresh, often topped with a sprinkling of peanuts. Excess supplies go towards making duck's blood pudding (see page 191).

BANGKOK, THAILAND

Chicken's blood pudding

Duck's blood pudding

Chicken feet

If one were looking for the Asian version of the kebab —
that post-alcohol grease-fest enjoyed by many British
revellers after a night out on the town — then this could
be it: deep-fried chicken feet (with salad), sold from
late-night food stalls throughout Asia. In fact, chicken
feet feature in the cuisines of a wide range of countries,
including China, much of South-East Asia, Jamaica, Peru
and South Africa. Depending on the location, they're eaten
steamed, boiled, grilled or in a soup; they also make an
excellent stock. However, being mostly skin, cartilage and
tendon, they are yet another acquired taste.

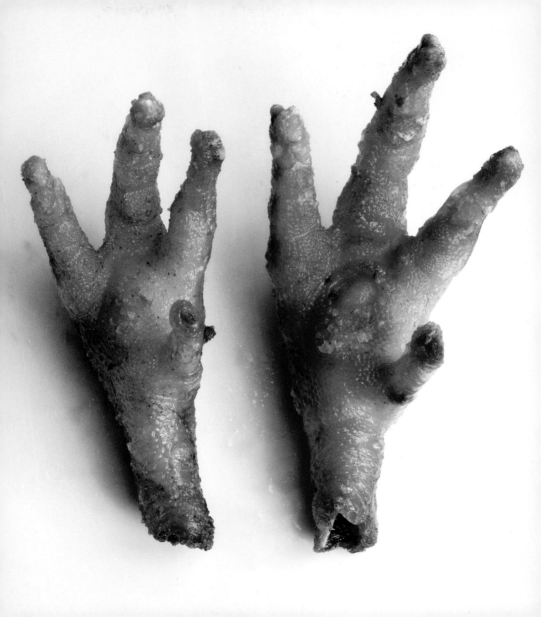

Chicken gizzards

Grilled chicken gizzards are a popular street food throughout South-East Asia. In other parts of the world, gizzards are used to make soups, casseroles and curries. In Potterville, Michigan, they even celebrate with the annual Gizzard Fest.

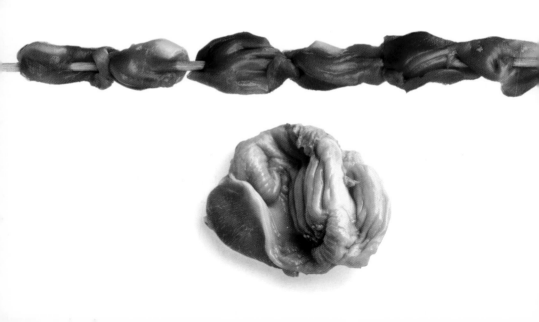

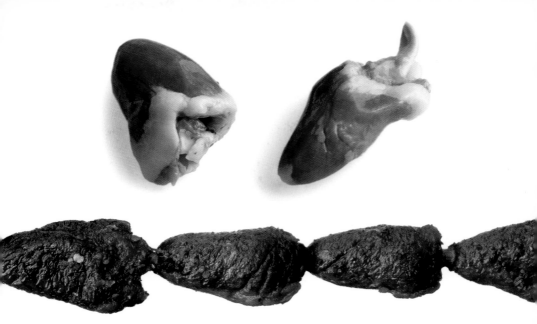

Chicken hearts

Packed with protein, vitamins and minerals, chicken hearts — shown here both raw and deep-fried with chilli flakes — also come in handy bite-sized pieces. They are eaten in various forms all over the world.

Cockscomb

In Italian cuisine, the cockscomb of a rooster (opposite) is an important ingredient in *cibrèo*, a traditional sauce consisting of various parts of the bird. In France, it's sometimes used as a rather novel garnish.

SINGAPORE

Chicken heads

Spicy grilled chicken heads are another popular late-night food in South-East Asia. With little actual meat on them, however, it's all about sucking, gnawing and the crunch.

Barbecued duck's tongue

Duck entrails

If the colour doesn't put you off, then the smell just might: this supermarket-prepared portion of duck entrails, complete with a sachet of orange sauce, has a somewhat, shall we say, 'distinct' aroma. Eaten in several other South-East Asian countries, duck entrails are often used to make soup. In Chinese restaurants, they are sometimes braised and served as part of an 'all-duck banquet', a feast consisting of up to thirty different duck-based dishes.

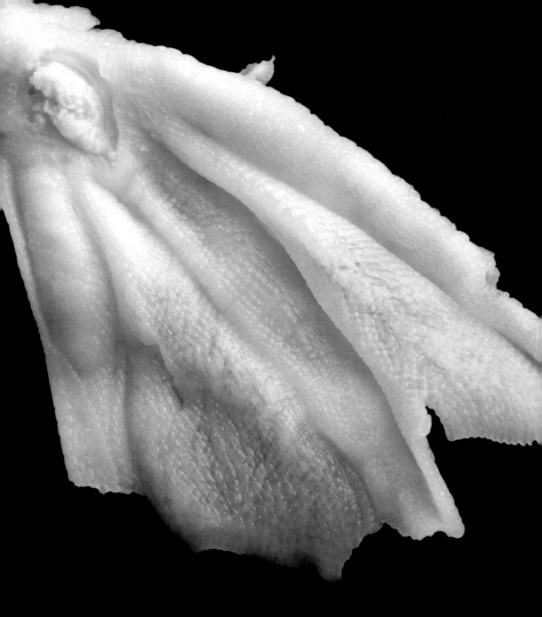

Deboned duck feet

This particular foot, semi-translucent and rather fragile-looking, was bought from a popular Thai supermarket, prepacked with several others. However, duck feet can also be found In China, where they are sometimes eaten in dim sum as an alternative to chicken feet (see page 192).

SERVING SUGGESTION

Blanch some duck feet in a mixture of water, spring onions and rice wine. Sauté some onion and fermented black beans until fragrant. Add some chopped green pepper, a chopped red chilli and the duck feet, and stir-fry. Mix in some oyster sauce, cook briefly, and serve.

Emu jerky

Just like the kangaroo (see page 117), the emu — the unofficial national bird of Australia — was once an important source of food for the Aborigines, who would pluck and gut the animal before cooking it on an open fire. Today, emus are farmed commercially, not only for meat but also for leather and oil. As food, emu is both low in fat and high in protein, the best cuts coming from the leg.

Emu jerky is delicious, much softer in texture than the beef variety. While it's mostly aimed at humans, emu jerky is also marketed as a gourmet snack for dogs.

Pigeon

Never a people knowingly to shy away from what's what in their cooking, the Vietnamese sometimes display a wry sense of humour. This roast pigeon's head was presented to me as part of a plate of spicy pigeon stir-fry, the bird's crispy little cranium protruding from a perfect mountain of rice. Looking like something out of a regal medieval banquet, the dish brought a smile to everyone it passed.

While consumption of the head appears to be limited to Asia, the rest of the bird is widely eaten throughout Europe, in some Middle Eastern nations and elsewhere. In 1862 a recipe for pigeon compote appeared in an issue of *Godey's Lady's Book*, a popular women's magazine published in the United States.

Deep-fried sparrow

Sold at the same gruesome 'pick 'n' mix' stall from which I bought the stir-fried tarantula and snake on a stick (see pages 39 and 170 respectively), deep-fried sparrow is another excellent example of the you-get-what-you-see school of cooking: it's a sparrow, and it's been deep-fried. So eat it.

Bought by the weight, the tiny sparrows can be finished off in one or two bites: perfect as a snack, they don't make much of a meal. If you're lucky, you might even get one of them to stand up on your plate …

Sparrows on a stick

If you like your fast food to resemble something out of one of the *Alien* movies, then Beijing is the place to go. Here, the raw birds are impaled on skewers before being deep-fried in hot oil flavoured with spices.

Woodcock

A popular game bird in parts of Europe, the United States and Japan, the woodcock is traditionally roasted without being gutted: the entrails are said to add to the essence of the bird's flavour. It's not only the woodcock's meat that is sought after, however: brushes made from the bird's pin feathers are highly prized by artists, especially for detailed work.

In the United Kingdom, breeding populations have been falling in recent years, partly because of overhunting, but also because of the erosion of the woodcock's natural habitat. The Royal Society for the Protection of Birds has placed the woodcock on its 'amber' list of species under threat.

LEFTOVERS

Battered hotdog and chips

Who needs a plate to eat off, or even a bag to hold?
In Seoul, South Korea, this meal on a stick is the ultimate
takeaway fast food for local students. It consists of
one hotdog sausage coated in dough, which is then
battered with crinkle-cut chips. The only effort required
is deciding whether to have it with ketchup or mustard.

Bird's nest soup

Eaten throughout South-East Asia, China and in Asian communities worldwide, bird's nest soup is made from the home of the appropriately named edible-nest swiftlet. Uniquely, the swiftlet's nest is composed of strands of its own saliva, which hardens when exposed to air. Traditionally, the nests were taken from the caves in which the birds live, an extremely hazardous occupation; increasingly, they're harvested from purpose-built nesting houses.

Famously, bird's nest soup is one of the most expensive foodstuffs in the world, with boxes of nests selling for hundreds of dollars. However, it's fair to say that the price has more to do with the dish's exclusivity and supposed health benefits than its taste. Although it's more soup-like than the shark-fin variety (see page 85), it has a rather thin, unremarkable flavour when eaten on its own.

Bird's nest tonic

If they can make it, they can bottle it. Promoted along the same lines as certain 'friendly bacteria' health drinks, miniature bottles of bird's nest tonic — in both sweetened and unsweetened varieties — are a daily must for many in South-East Asia and China. Also available in packs of six, twelve and twenty-four.

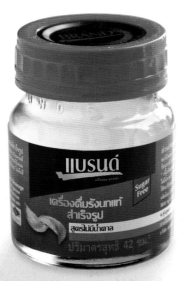

Century egg

According to legend, century eggs are prepared by soaking a batch of eggs in horse urine. Considering their pungent, ammonia-rich odour, that story seems quite plausible. In fact, century eggs — also known as preserved eggs, hundred-year eggs and thousand-year eggs — are made by preserving duck or chicken eggs in a mixture of clay, ash, salt, lime and rice husks or straw for several months (not years). The result is like nothing else on Earth: the yolk becomes a dark-green goo, while the white is transformed into a dark-brown, translucent jelly.

Century eggs are widely available all over Asia, where they are extremely popular. They can be eaten on their own, and are sometimes used as an ingredient in other dishes, such as century-egg congee (diced century egg, chicken and rice porridge).

CHINATOWN, BANGKOK, THAILAND

Chinese rice dumplings

Available in a range of colours, including red and pink,
these flattened dumplings – similar to *jiaozi*, another type
of Chinese dumpling – come stuffed with meat and/or
vegetables. The thin pastry used for the casings is made
from rice flour.

Crispy bird's nest

This deep-fried fast-food product is allegedly made from the same nests as used for bird's nest soup (see page 219). However, its relatively low price would suggest that this claim has more to do with marketing than with the truth.

Deep-fried Mars bar

Don't try this at home. Often thought to be nothing more than an urban myth, the deep-fried Mars bar is very much a reality. Sold as a novelty item in many Scottish fish-and-chip shops, this calorific confection is made by deep-frying a Mars bar coated in batter. However, it's not as easy as one might think: the key is to use a room-temperature Mars bar, cold batter and extremely hot fat — hence the health-and-safety warning. The balance between crispiness and gooeyness depends on the length of cooking; either way, the result is almost certainly life-shortening. In the interests of variety, the Scots have extended the range of foods cooked in this style to include pies, pizza and Creme Eggs.

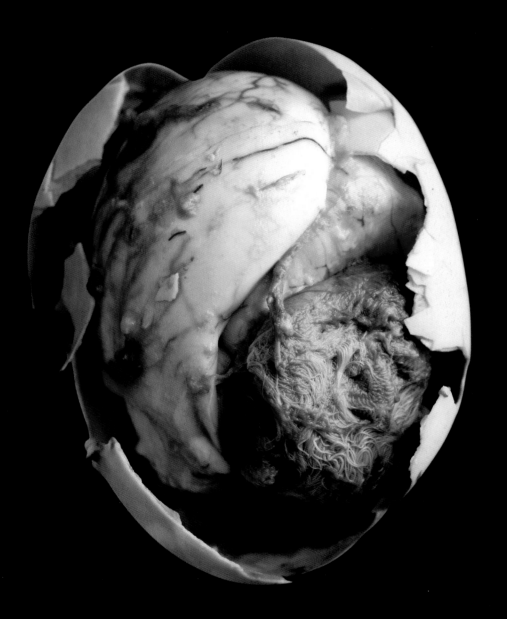

Balut

If you fancy a mouthful of feathers, barely formed bone and duck embryo, then *balut* is definitely the dish for you. For many South-East Asians — especially the people of the Philippines — this boiled fertilized duck egg is the street food *par excellence*. Widely believed to be an aphrodisiac, *balut* is usually eaten as it comes, perhaps with a pinch of salt. After making a hole in the top of the egg, one sips the liquid first before consuming the rest of the contents. The preferred age of the egg is a matter of geography. Filipinos consider them at their best at seventeen days old, before the feathers and bones have fully developed, while the Vietnamese prefer them a few days older, by which time the embryo is recognizable as a baby duck.

Haggis

While the exact origins of haggis remain a little unclear, only a fool would question its status as Scotland's national dish — especially when in Scotland itself. Essentially, haggis consists of minced sheep's innards (including heart, stomach, spleen and lungs) — mixed with fat, oatmeal, stock and seasoning — encased and cooked in yet another part of the animal's gut. Traditionally, haggis is served with 'neeps and tatties', swede or turnip and potatoes.

Haggis is also probably one of only a handful of foods to have inspired poetry. Written by Robert Burns in 1786, 'Address to a Haggis' is customarily recited after the entrance of the dish during a Burns supper, a celebration of the life and work of the poet. The second line of Burns's poem describes haggis as the 'Great chieftain o' the pudding-race!'.

Nattō

Sticky, smelly, slimy and with an unpleasant aftertaste, *nattō* is all you could possibly want from a breakfast food … if you live in Japan, that is. Consisting of fermented soy beans, *nattō* is a traditional Japanese dish eaten in all parts of the country, often in the morning but also at other times of the day. It may have its bad points (even some Japanese don't like it), but it is at least good for you.

Sources differ over the origins of *nattō*, but one story claims it was accidentally discovered by a group of soldiers in medieval Japan. Attacked while boiling some soy beans, they quickly packed the beans in straw bags and fled. When they came to open the bags a few days later, they discovered that the beans had fermented, but ate them anyway. Today, *nattō* is widely available in small polystyrene containers, sometimes with a sachet of soy sauce or other flavouring, and is often eaten with rice. It's also used as an accompaniment for raw quail eggs.

Salted duck egg

Salted duck eggs are a staple Chinese preserved food made by soaking the eggs in brine or coating them with salted charcoal. Typically, the eggs are boiled or steamed before being used as a flavouring in other dishes. The preservation process produces a very salty egg white, and a rich, vibrant, orange-red yolk. The latter is sometimes added to Chinese mooncakes to symbolize the moon.

Although Chinese in origin, salted duck eggs are also produced in a number of South-East Asian countries, including Thailand, Malaysia and the Philippines. If they were produced in the West, they would undoubtedly be accompanied by a health warning: a typical 70-g (2 1/2-oz) egg contains more than the recommended daily amount of cholesterol.

Stargazy pie

Stargazy pie is a traditional Cornish dish containing baked sardines that have been arranged so that their heads, and sometimes tails, are pointing skywards. While the vertical positioning of the fish is common to all recipes, some use mackerel or herring instead of sardines. Most versions also include hard-boiled eggs, bacon, onion and mustard.

The history of stargazy pie can be traced to the Cornish village of Mousehole and the story of Tom Bawcock, a fisherman who is said to have saved the village from famine by bringing home his catch during a storm. Tom's heroic efforts are commemorated on Tom Bawcock's Eve, a festival held on 23 December each year during which residents of Mousehole put on a lantern procession and eat stargazy pie, supposedly the dish eaten after the fisherman's return from the sea.

THE ONES THAT GOT AWAY

Inevitably, any catalogue or collection will contain omissions, and this book – a personal selection of foods that I found interesting and/or photogenic – is no exception. The following are just some of the foodstuffs I heard about during my research but, for one reason or another, wasn't able to taste or photograph: antelope (South Africa); ants' eggs (Laos and Thailand); bison (South Africa); budgie (Europe); cat (China and Vietnam); elephant (northern Thailand, but only if the animal has died from natural causes); fruit bats (Thailand); honey ants (Australia); horse (France); lambs' lungs (Europe, the Middle East and Africa); mice (Asia); monkey brains (Africa); peacock (Classical Rome); puffin (Iceland and the Faroe Islands); squirrel (United Kingdom, but only the grey variety); and sweetbreads (the thymus and pancreas gland of a calf or lamb; Europe, the United States and the Middle East). Subjects for the next edition, perhaps?

FURTHER READING

Alan Davidson, *The Oxford Companion to Food*, Oxford (Oxford University Press) 1999

M.F.K. Fisher, *How to Cook a Wolf* [1942], New York (North Point Press) 1988

Stefan Gates, *Gastronaut*, London (BBC) 2005

Jerry Hopkins, *Extreme Cuisine*, London (Bloomsbury) 2005

Larousse Gastronomique, rev. edn, London (Hamlyn) 2001

产品说明
Product Directions

袁府驴肉

正宗特产

INGREDIENTS:
CAMEL, SOY BEANS,
WHEAT, SALT,
LEMON JUICE,
SPICES

Manufactured in the
Northern Territory, Australia a
The Territory Jerky Factory

Territory Jerky Pty Ltd
1 Milner Road

NATURAL JELLYFISH HEAD
イソスタンドクラゲ

香辣味
PIQUANT

海蜇头

即食

福州恒兴旺水产有限公司 净含量: 150克 NET WT 150g
Fuzhou Heng Xiang Wang Aquatic Co., Ltd. 固形物含量≥70% Solid Content

THỊT
CHÓ
SỐ 5 CHỢ GẠO (CŨ)